Vidya Sinha's Cookbook Indian Vegetarian Recipes of Bhojpur

Vidya Sinha

Vidya Sinha's Cookbook: Indian Vegetarian Recipes of Bhojpur

© 2011 Vidya Sinha

ISBN: 978-1-61170-050-3

Photographs: Binita Sinha-Sharma, Vidya Sinha

Concept & Design: Prabhakar Aloka, Amitabh Divakar

Translation: Binita Sinha-Sharma

All rights reserved. No part of this publication may be reproduced, stored in a retrieval system or transmitted in any form or by any means, electronic, mechanical, photocopies, recording or otherwise, without the prior written consent of the author.

Printed in the USA and UK on acid-free paper.

To order additional copies of this book go to:
www.rp-author.com/Sinha

Robertson Publishing™
59 North Santa Cruz Avenue
Los Gatos, California 95030 USA
www.RobertsonPublishing.com

Contents

- 6 — Gobi Mussalam (Cauliflower Whole)
- 10 — Besan Kharera (Chickpea squares in curry)
- 12 — Kharera Curry
- 14 — Besan Dhokha (Chickpea potatoes)
- 16 — Besan Dhokha (Chickpea potatoes) contd.
- 18 — Karhi-Bari
- 22 — Panchranga sabji (Five vegetables)
- 24 — Bhindi Rasedaar (Okra in gravy)
- 26 — Baigan–Vadi (Eggplant with nuggets)
- 30 — Lauki with Panchforan (Bottle gourd with five spices)
- 32 — Konhra (Pumpkin)
- 34 — Baingan, Palak saag (Eggplant with spinach)
- 36 — Saag (Swiss chard)
- 38 — Chawlai saag (Amaranth green)
- 40 — Poi saag (Climbing spinach or Malabar spinach) with potatoes
- 42 — Bathua Saag (Chenopodium green)
- 44 — Karela Kalonji (Stuffed Bitter Gourd)
- 46 — Baingan Kalonji (Eggplant fried)
- 48 — Bhindi Masala (Okra spicy)
- 50 — Bhindi Bhujia (Okra fry)
- 52 — Aloo bhujia (Potato fry)
- 56 — Makuni (Sattu Paratha)

58	Litti
62	Peetha Chana Dal
66	Dal bahri Poori (Chana dal stuffed bread)
68	Dal pithi (wheat dumplings in cooked lentil)
72	Papra (Cheela) Pancake
74	Poori Plain
76	Kachaouri Savory
78	Pulao
82	Kachalu (Potatoes with Yogurt)
84	Lauki Raita
86	Aloo Chokha (Mashed potatoes)
88	Sattu Chokha (Spicy)
90	Baingan Chokha (Mashed eggplant)
92	Tamatar Chokha (Mashed Tomatoes)
94	Chana Bajka
98	Pua
100	Sohan Halwa (Sweet Gram Squares)
102	Perakiya of khoya (Stuffed Sweet Pastry)
104	Gond Laddu
106	Narial Pua (Coconut filled pastry)
111	Basic Curry

Metric Conversion Chart

Volume Measurement (Dry)

1 teaspoon (tsp.) = 5 mL

1 tablespoon (tbs.) = 15 mL

1/2 cup = 125 mL

1 cup = 250 mL

Volume Measurement (Fluid)

1 fluid ounce (oz.) (2 tbs) = 30 mL

8 fluid oz. (1 cup) = 240 mL

Weight (mass)

1 oz.= 30 g

8 oz.= 225 g

16 oz. = 450 g = 1 pound

Introduction

Indian cuisine reflects the diversity of the subcontinent as recipes incorporate the basic ingredients and staples in a way that is unique to every region. This cookbook is a collection of everyday vegetarian recipes based on the culinary traditions of Bhojpur region in north India.

Bhojpur region comprises parts of the south Gangetic plain extending over the west Bihar and east Uttar Pradesh states, as such, it shares the rich historic and cultural traditions with the rest of the plain and north India.

This region evolved as an agrarian belt and is one of the most densely populated areas of India. The folk cuisines of this region are simple, wholesome, and full of flavor. Rice, wheat flour, gram flour (besan), yellow pigeon pea (chana dal), kala chana (Bengal gram) are the basic staples. Flour made of roasted kala chana, known as Sattu, is very popular in Bhojpur and all over Bihar. Preparations like Litti, Dal-Pithi, Dal Bahri Puri, can be a complete meal if served with a combination of vegetables and yogurt. Traditional everyday recipes are thus very healthy.

Most recipes call for mustard oil, or ghee (clarified butter), as cooking medium and the cooking process requires fewer utensils.

The following page presents a list of the most common ingredients used in this cookbook and their English name.

Cereals
Atta (Wheat flour)
Besan (Chickpea/ Gram flour)
Sattu (Roasted Chana flour)
Maida (all purpose wheat flour)
Sooji (Cream of wheat)

Pulses/Lentil
Chana dal (Pigeon pea)
Moong dal (Yellow lentil)
Kala chana (Bengal gram)
Masoor dal (Red lentil)

Vegetables
Bhindi (Okra)
Lal Saag (Swiss chard)
Baingan (Eggplant)
Tamatar (Tomato)
Pyaj (Onion)
Adrak (Ginger)
Lahsun (Garlic)
Gobi (Cauliflower)
Palak (Spinach)
Mooli (Radish)
Bathua saag

Dhania patta (Green coriander leaves/ cilantro)
Poi saag (Climbing spinach/Malabar spinach)

Spices
Methi (Fenugreek)
Haldi (Turmeric)
Dhania (Coriander)
Hing (Asafoetida)
Kalonji/Mangrail (Negella)
Saunf (Fennel)
Mirch (Chili)
Jeera (Cumin)
Ajwain (Carom)

Panchforan (Five seeds- methi, jeera, saunf, ajwain, Kalonji mixed together)

Garam masala (mix of fragrant powdered spices- cardamom, cinnamon, mace, pepper, nutmeg, & clove)

This cookbook is a result of years of experience and the basic learning I had from my mother and grandmother. My initial learning came very naturally as I started assisting my mother in her kitchen when I was in my early teens. Fond memories of my mother's, grandmother's and aunt's kitchen still linger in my mind. In my later years, I learned from my mother-in-law and from my late husband Radhika Raman Prasad Sinha who always encouraged me and provided feedback to improvise my recipes while preserving the fundamentals of the Bhojpur style.

Cooking for my grandsons — Aishwarya and Vaibhav, has been one of my greatest joys. They both have their own favorite dishes. In recent years, I had the opportunity to share many of these recipes with my daughter-in-law — Mita. I am able to compile these recipes due to the encouragement received from my children - Prabhakar, Amitabh, and Binita as well as from my brothers - Ravi, Bharat, and Kaushal, Deepak and his wife Shipra. I thank my son-in-law — Anoop, who tested and provided feedback on several dishes as I was preparing for this publication.

Though the geographic identity of the Bhojpur region is defined by the west Bihar and east Uttar Pradesh regions in India, people from Bhojpur have settled almost in every continent where they try to maintain and celebrate the customary traditions. In my humble way I am trying to reach them and present them the traditional recipes.

This book is organized into sub-sections, the first one being curried dishes, followed by vegetables, poori (bread) and main-course, then side-dishes, and lastly sweet dishes.

I hope that my personal collection of everyday recipes from Bhojpur will serve well those interested in Indian regional vegetarian cooking.

August, 2011   *Vidya Sinha*

Part - 1
Curried Preparations
(Rassedar Tarkari)

Karhi-Bari

Panchranga Tarkari

Gobi Mussalam

and more...

Gobi Mussalam (Cauliflower Whole)

Ingredients

Cauliflower – 1
Tomato (thinly sliced) – 2 cups
Onion – 2 cups (thinly sliced) & 1/2 cup (chopped)
Garlic (chopped) – 1 1/2 tbs
Ginger (chopped) – 2 tbs
Cumin seed – 1/2 tsp
Red chili – 1 large whole
Green cardamom – 1 pod
Black cardamom - 1 pod
Cloves whole – 3
Bay leaves - 2
Cinnamon stick – 1 small
Mace – 1 small
Garam masala powder – 1/2 tsp
Coriander powder – 1/2 tsp
Cumin powder – 1/2 tsp
Turmeric powder – 1 tsp
Desiccated coconut paste – 4 tbs
Peanut (ground nut) paste – 4 tbs
Salt to taste
Oil – 4 tbs
Ghee (clarified butter) – 1 tsp
Coriander (cilantro) leaves – 1/4 cup (chopped)

Method

1. Heat 4 tbs oil in a heavy bottom pan, add cumin seeds, and wait for the seeds to turn brown.

2. Add green and black cardamoms, cloves, bay leaves, cinnamon stick, and mace. Stir well for 30 seconds.

3. Add chopped ginger and garlic, and 1/2 cups of chopped onions. Fry the mixture till onions turn golden brown.

4. Except Garam masala, add the powdered spices (coriander, cumin, and turmeric) mix with 2 tbs water and stir with the onion mixture for 1 minute.

5. Add the sliced onions (2 cups) and chopped tomatoes. Fry for 2 minutes.

6. Add the paste of coconut and peanut (ground nut). Fry for 2 more minutes.

7. Add 1 cup water to make a thick gravy.

8. Now add the gram masala powder and salt to taste.

9. *Heat 1 tsp ghee (clarified butter) in a wide 16 quart pan. Place the whole cauliflower head, stem side down, in the heated oil and pour the gravy on it making sure that the gravy evenly spreads over and around the cauliflower*

10. *Cover and cook for about 10 minutes on low heat. After 10 minutes check to see if the cauliflower is fork-tender (the fork will slide into it with gentle pressure). If too firm, cook for another 5 minutes and check with fork again. Be careful not to overcook otherwise the cauliflower will turn mushy.*

11. *To serve, carefully place the cauliflower on a platter, top with gravy and garnish with chopped coriander (cilantro) leaves.*

Besan Kharera (Chickpea squares in curry)

Ingredients

Besan (chickpea flour) - 1 cup
Turmeric powder - 1/2 tsp
Cumin powder - 1/2 tsp
Chili powder - 1/4 tsp
Fresh coriander (cilantro) leaves chopped - 2 tbs
Salt - to taste
Ajwain - 1/2 tsp
Carrot (finely grated) - 2 tbs
Cabbage (finely grated) - 2 tbs
Ginger paste - 1/2 tbs
Garam masala - 1/2 tsp
Oil for pan frying

Method

1. Mix Besan (chickpea flour) with water to get a consistency of pancake batter. Make sure there are no lumps.

2. In a deep pan, heat 1 tbs oil, add ajwain and wait for it to sizzle, then add the besan mixture and the chopped carrot and chopped cabbage. Mix well.

3. As the mixture heats it will thicken. Keep stirring. After a few minutes when it gets to a dough-like consistency and does not stick to the pan, remove it from the stove.

4. Grease a cookie pan or a metal tray with a little oil and spread the mixture into a 1 inch thick layer. You may use a greased rolling pin to spread it. Let it cool for about an hour. Cut into square pieces.

5. Heat oil in a frying pan and pan-fry the pieces to a golden brown color.

6. It can be served with chutney or tomato ketchup or can be made into Kahrera curry. (Recipe on the next page)

Kharera Curry

Ingredients

Besan Kharera pieces (recipe from the previous page)

Onion paste – 2 tbs
Garlic paste – 1 tsp
Ginger paste – 1/2 tsp
Cumin powder – 1 tsp
Turmeric powder – 1 tsp
Chili powder - 1/2 tsp
Garam masala powder –1/2 tsp
Cumin seeds – 1/2 tsp
Onions finely chopped – 2 tbs
Tomatoes chopped – 1/2 cup
Coriander leaves (cilantro) chopped – 2 tbs
Salt to taste

Method

1. Heat oil in a deep pan, add cumin seeds and let it sizzle.

2. Add chopped onions and fry it to a light brown color.

3. Add all the dry ingredients except the Garam masala powder, and fry till the water evaporates and you get the aroma of fried spices.

4. Add chopped tomatoes and fry till it incorporates well, then add 1 cup of water to make gravy. Let it boil and thicken.

5. Add the kharera pieces. Boil for 2-3 minutes then turn off the stove. Add the Gram masala powder and salt.

6. Garnish with chopped coriander (cilantro) leaves. This can be served with rice or chapati.

Besan Dhokha (Chickpea potatoes)

Ingredients

For Chickpea potatoes

Besan (Gram flour) – 1.5 cup
Cumin seeds – 1/4 tsp
Turmeric powder – 1/4 tsp
Cinnamon powder – ¼ tsp
Eno powder – 1 tsp
Gram Masala powder – 1/4 tsp
Yogurt – 4 tbs.
Salt to taste
Oil – 3 tbs.

Method

1. In a mixing bowl, add the besan and 2 tbs oil, all spices and salt, and mix well.

2. Adding yogurt (about one tbs) at a time, make a dough of the besan. It will be dense and a bit sticky. Divide it into 10 equal parts.

3. Rub a few drops of oil on the palms of your hand and make small balls (1 – 1.5 inch diameter) of the besan dough. Shape it like small potatoes (hence the name.)

4. In a deep pot, boil 1.5 liters water and add the besan dough balls. Keep them boiling for about 20-25 minutes. These will swell a little bit and float.

5. Turn off the heat and remove the besan balls let them cool then cut each of them into quarters.

6. Heat the remaining 1 tbs. oil in a frying pan and pan-fry the pieces. Now you can put these pieces in curry. (Recipe on the next page.)

Besan Dhokha (Chickpea potatoes) contd.

Ingredients for Curry

Onion paste - 4 tbs
Ginger paste - 1.5 tbs.
Garlic paste - 1 tbs
Chili powder - 1 tsp
Turmeric powder - 1/2 tsp
Coriander powder - 1 tbs
Pepper corn whole - 1/4 tsp
Fennel seed -1/4 tsp
Cumin seed - 1/4 tsp
Bay leaves - 2 pieces
Garam masala powder - 1 tsp
Tomato (chopped) - 1/2 cup
Onion (chopped) - 4 tbs
Oil - 5 tbs
Ghee (clarified butter) - 1 tbs
Water - 1 cup
Coriander leaves (chopped) - 2 tbs
Salt to taste

Method

For Curry

1. Heat 5 tbs oil in wok. Add bay leaves, and cumin seed. Let it turn light brown. Add chopped onions and fry it to a golden brown color.

2. Add all the powdered spices, garlic, ginger paste, clarified butter and fry them for 7-8 minutes till they no longer stick to the pan.

3. Add chopped tomatoes. Mix well and let it cook for 5 minutes.

4. Add the pieces of chickpea potatoes, 1 cup water, mix well. Add salt to taste.

5. Cover and simmer for 10 minutes. Remove from stove. Add the garam masala powder. Garnish with chopped coriander leaves and serve with rice or chapati.

Karhi-Bari

Ingredients

Besan - 1 1/4 cups
Yogurt – ½ cup
Turmeric powder – ½ tsp
Methi (fenugreek seed) – ¼ tsp
Cumin seed - ½ tsp
Red chili whole – 1 piece
Hing (asafoetida) – 1 pinch
Oil – ½ cup
Ghee (Clarified butter) - 1 tsp
Salt – to taste

Bari

1. Keep 1/4 cup besan aside.

2. Take remaining besan in a deep bowl, add enough water to make a paste of it. Using a hand blender and a little water, mix it at medium speed for two minutes. The mixture will become light and airy.

3. Take a cup of water and put one drop of besan paste into it, if it floats then the mixture is ready. (see the picture on the opposite page). If not, mix it a little longer and test again.

4. Add the cumin seed and salt to this mixture and stir well.

5. Heat oil in a wok. With a teaspoon, drop the mixture in the oil a spoon at a time. These will puff-up and float in the oil. Turn down heat and fry these to a light golden color. Remove from wok and set these bari aside.

Karhi

1. In a blender, mix the remaining 1/4 cup besan with two cups water, turmeric, and yogurt.

2. In a large crock-pot, heat 2 tbs oil, add the hing, methi, and the whole red chili.

3. Pour the besan-yogurt mixture into the hot seasoned oil. It will start to thicken. Keep stirring. Bring it to boil once then add bari.

4. Keep stirring and allow the karhi liquid to a boil again. Reduce heat and let it simmer for 10-15 minutes so that the besan is cooked the and bari pieces are softened

5. In a small ladle heat the Ghee, add hing and 1/2 tsp cumin seeds. Allow them to turn brown. Pour over the karhi-bari. Serve it with rice and aloo bhujia.

Panchranga sabji (Five vegetables)

Ingredients

Vegetables- the following should be cut in one-inch cubes:
  Potato – 2 cups
  Eggplants – 2 cups
  Beans – 1 cup
  Radish – ½ cup
  Sweet peas – ½ cup

Tomato (finely chopped) – ½ cup
Coriander leaves – ¼ cup
Methi (fenugreek seeds) – 1 tsp
Red chili (dry) – 1 piece
Garlic (minced) – 1 tbs
Turmeric powder – 1 tbs
Oil – 2 tbs
Salt – to taste
Water – 2 cups

Method

1. Heat oil in a wok, add fenugreek seeds and let it turn brown.

2. Add garlic and fry till it turns light brown, add the red chili and green peas, fry for a minute.

3. Add potatoes, beans, radish, sweet peas and eggplant along with salt, turmeric, and 2 cups of water. Stir, cover and cook till the potatoes are tender but not mushy.

4. Add tomatoes. Cover and cook till the tomatoes are done and assimilated. Turn off heat. Garnish with the chopped coriander.

Bhindi Rasedaar (Okra in gravy)

Ingredients

Bhindi (Okra) – 200 grams
Tomato – 1 small
Fenugreek seeds – 1/2 tsp
Mustard powder – 1 tbs
Coriander powder – 1 tbs
Turmeric powder – 1/2 tbs
Garlic paste – 1 tbs
Chili powder – 1/4 tsp (optional)
Oil - 4 tbs
Water - 1 cup
Salt – to taste
Coriander (cilantro) leaves chopped – 2 tbs.

Method

1. Clean bhindi and cut into pieces about 2 inches long. See picture on the opposite page.

2. Heat 2 tablespoons oil in a wok and pan-fry the bhindis to a golden brown color. Remove bhindis and set them aside.

3. Add remaining 2 tbs oil in the wok, add the methi, wait till it turns brown then add all powdered spices and the garlic paste with two tbs water. Fry the spices to a golden brown color.

4. Add 1 cup water, and tomatoes to the fried spices and bring it to boil to make gravy. Add fried bhindis and salt to the gravy and cook till the gravy thickens.

5. Remove from heat. Garnish with chopped coriander leaves and serve with rice or chapati.

Baigan–Vadi (Eggplant with nuggets)

Ingredients

Baingan (eggplant, cut into cubes) – 6 cups
Vadi (nuggets of lentil) – ½ cup
Methi (fenugreek seeds) – ½ tsp
Hing (asafoetida) – 1 pinch
Turmeric – 1 tsp
Salt – to taste
Oil – 4 tbs
Red chili – 1 piece (optional)

Method

1. Heat 2 tbs oil in a wok, add the vadi (nuggets) and stir-fry till the nuggets are light brown. Remove the nuggets and set them aside.

2. In the same wok, heat the remaining 2 tbs oil, add hing, methi seeds, and red chili (optional). Let methi seeds turn light brown.

3. Add the chopped eggplants, salt and turmeric, stir well for few minutes till the eggplants start to cook.

4. Add the stir-fried vadi and water. Cover and simmer till the vadi and eggplants are cooked.

Part - 2
Saag, Bhujia etc.

Bhindi Bhujia

Palak Baingan Saag

Aaloo Bhujia

and more...

Lauki with Panchforan
(Bottle gourd with five spices)

Ingredients

Lauki (finely chopped) – 4 cups
Oil – 1 tbs
Panchforan – 1 tsp (see the note below)
Tejpatta (bay leaf) – 1 piece
Hing (asafoetida) – 1 pinch
Turmeric – 1/2 tsp
Red chili whole - 1 piece (optional)
Salt to taste.
Sugar - 1/2 tsp (optional)

Note: Panchforan is five seeds - methi (fenugreek), saunf (fennel), sarson (mustard), ajwain (carom) and kalonji (nigella), all mixed in equal quantities. You can mix them in a small bowl first and take one tsp for this recipe.

Method

1. Heat oil in a pan, add tejpatta (bay leaf), hing, and panchforan and red chili (if using). Wait till the seeds start to crackle.

2. Add chopped lauki, salt, turmeric and the optional sugar. Incorporate well. Cover the pan.

3. Turn down heat to a medium low and let it simmer for 10-15 minutes till the water from lauki evaporates and the lauki is cooked properly. It will change to translucent yellow color.

4. Remove the cooked lauki from heat and serve with Poori or chapati.

Konhra (Pumpkin)

Ingredients

Konhra (pumpkin) peeled and chopped – 4 cups
Methi (fenugreek seeds) 1 tsp
Hing (asafoetida) – a pinch
Red chili (whole) – 1 piece (optional)
Gur (jaggery) – 1 tbs
Oil – 2 tbs
Salt – to taste
Amchoor (mango powder) – 1 tsp Or Lime juice – 2 tbs

Method

1. Heat oil in a wok, add hing, methi, and red chili (optional.)

2. Let them sizzle till the methi seeds turn light brown.

3. Add chopped pumpkin along with salt, stir and let it simmer till the pumpkin is softened.

4. Add gur and let it cook uncovered till the water evaporates. Remove from heat.

5. Stir in amchoor or lime juice. If desired, garnish with green coriander leaves.

Baingan, Palak saag (Eggplant with spinach)

Ingredients

Spinach (washed, and chopped) – 6 cups
Eggplant (cut in small cubes) – 2 cups
Methi (fenugreek seeds) – ½ tsp
Hing (asafoetida) – 1 pinch
Oil – 1 tbs
Salt – to taste
Red chili – 1 piece (optional)

Method

1. *Heat oil in a wok, add hing, methi, and red chili (optional).*

2. *Add chopped eggplants and stir well. The eggplant will change its color to light brown.*

3. *Add spinach, and salt; stir to mix well.*

4. *Turn down heat, cover and cook till the extra liquid evaporates.*

Saag (Swiss chard)

Ingredients

Red Saag (swiss chard) Chopped – 6 cups
Chana daal (pigeon pea) – 4 tbs
(You may use soaked Bengal grams (kala chana) as well.)

Onion (finely chopped) – 2 tbs
Methi (fenugreek seed) – ½ tsp
Jeera (cumin seed) -1/2 tsp
Salt- to taste
Oil – 2 tbs
Red chili – 1 piece (optional)

Method

1. Heat oil in a deep pan or a wok, add cumin seeds and when the seeds crackle, add the methi seeds and red chili (optional). Wait for it to turn light brown then add chopped onions.

2. Fry till the onions turn light brown then add the chana dal (or kala chana), and fry for a minute.

3. Add chopped saag to the onion-lentil mixture, add salt and ½ cup water.

4. Cover and simmer on medium-low heat till the extra liquid evaporates.

Chawlai saag (Amaranth green)

Ingredients

Chawlai (Amaranth green) chopped – 8 cups
Masoor daal (red lentil) soaked – 4 tbs .
(You may use soaked Bengal grams (kala chana) as well.)

Onion (finely chopped) – 1/2 cup
Jeera (cumin seed) -1/2 tsp
Ginger paste – 1/2 tsp
Salt- to taste
Oil – 3 tbs
Red chili – 1 piece (optional)

Method

1. Heat oil in a deep pan or a wok, add cumin seeds and when the seeds crackle, add red chili (optional).

2. Add the chopped onions. Fry till the onions turn light brown then add the ginger paste, red lentils (masoor dal), and fry for a minute.

3. Add copped saag to the onion-lentil mixture, add salt and ½ cup water.

4. Cover and simmer on medium-low heat till the extra liquid is absorbed.

Poi saag (Climbing spinach or Malabar spinach) with potatoes

Ingredients

Poi saag Chopped – 8 cup
Potato peeled and cut into small cubes – 1 cup
Methi (fenugreek seed) – ½ tsp
Haldi (turmeric powder) – ¼ tsp
Hing (asafoetida) – 1 pinch
Salt- to taste
Oil – 1 tbs
Red chili – 1 piece (optional)

Method

1. Heat oil in a deep pan or a wok, add fenugreek seeds , hing (asafoetida), add red chili (optional).

2. Add the chopped potatoes and turmeric. Fry till the potatoes turn light brown.

3. Add copped saag to the potatoes, salt and ½ cup water.

4. Cover and simmer on medium-low heat till the potatoes are cooked and extra liquid evaporates.

Bathua Saag (Chenopodium green)

Ingredients

Bathua saag (cleaned and chopped) – 10 cups
Green chili (finely chopped) – 1 piece
Ginger (finely chopped) – I inch piece
Garlic (minced) – 1 tbs
Salt- to taste
Mustard oil – 1 tbs

Method

1. Cook saag leaves in a pressure cooker. After the pressure builds, cook for five minutes under full pressure. Remove from heat and let it cool.

2. Remove the lid from pressure cooker and put it back on the stove, cook uncovered till the liquid evaporates and saag leaves are fully cooked.

3. After the cooked saag has cooled, put it in a blender and blend it into a thick paste.

4. Add the chopped spices, salt, and mustard oil. Mix well and serve with chapati or rice.

Karela Kalonji (Stuffed Bitter Gourd)

Ingredients

Karela (Bitter gourd) small size about 4" each – 300 grams
Bengal gram (Kala chana) soaked – ½ cup
Onion (finely chopped)- ½ cup
Mustard powder – 2 tbs
Coriander powder – 2 tbs
Turmeric powder – ½ tsp
Garlic paste – 1 tbs
Amchoor (mango powder) – 1 tbs
Methi (fenugreek seed) – ½ tsp
Oil – 4 tbs
Water – 1 cup
Salt – to taste

Method

1. Slit each of the karelas in the middle, be careful that it does not split apart.

2. Rub karelas with salt, and turmeric.

3. In a pressure cooker put the karelas and Bengal gram with one cup water and cook under full pressure for 2 minutes. Remove pressure cooker from heat and let it cool.

4. Using a small tsp, carefully scoop out the seeds and pulp from the karelas and keep them aside.

5. In a wok, heat 1 table spoon oil, add methi (fenugreek) seeds, let it crackle, then fry onions till onions turn light brown.

6. Add the reserved karela seeds and pulp to the onion mixture and fry for 1 minute. Add the remaining ingredients, except the amchoor (mango powder). Fry for 2 more minutes, turn-off heat, then add amchoor.

7. Fill each of the empty shells of karela with the above mixture. Make sure that the karelas maintain their shape.

8. Put remaining oil in a frying pan and lightly pan-fry each of the karelas to a golden brown color. Serve warm with rice or chapati.

Baingan Kalonji (Eggplant fried)

Ingredients

Baigan (eggplant) 4 inches long – 8
Tomato (chopped) or Amchoor (mango powder) - 1 tsp
Mustard powder - 2 tbs
Coriander powder - 2 tbs
Turmeric powder - 1 tsp
Chili powder - 1/2 tsp
Garlic paste - 1 tbs
Tomato chopped - 1/2 cup
Salt- to taste-
Oil - 4 tbs
Water - 1/2 cup

Note: This recipe is best for long tender eggplants of about 2" diameter and 4-5 inches long.

Method

1. Slit baingans (eggplant) lengthwise, make sure the pieces are attached to the crown. (See picture on the opposite page.)

2. Mix all spices and salt with a little water to make a thick paste.

3. In a deep wok, arrange the baingans in single layer and pour spice paste over it. Add 1/2 cup water to cover the layer of baingans and add salt.

4. Put a lid on the wok, reduce heat and let it simmer till the liquid evaporates. Baingans will be only half-cooked.

5. Add a little oil in a frying pan, carefully remove cooked baingans from the wok and pan fry to a golden brown color.

Bhindi Masala (Okra spicy)

Ingredient

Bhindi (okra)- 200 grams
Mustard powder – 1 tsp
Chili powder – 1/4 tsp
Turmeric – 1/2 tsp
Coriander powder - 1 tsp
Garlic paste – 1 tsp
Methi (fenugreek seeds) –1/4 tsp
Oil – 2 tbs
Salt – 2 tbs

Method

1. Clean and cut the bhindis into about 2 inches long pieces. If the bhindis are small, just slit in the middle and keep them whole. (See picture on the opposite page.)

2. Mix all powdered spices with garlic paste, and salt and rub it thoroughly over the bhindis, let it sit for a few minutes.

3. Heat oil in a frying pan, add the methi (fenugreek seeds) wait till it turns brown, add the bhindis and pan-fry them to a golden brown color.

Bhindi Bhujia (Okra fry)

Ingredients

Bhindi (okra) – 200 grams
Methi (fenugreek seeds) – 1 tsp
Oil – 2 tbs
Salt – to taste

Method

1. Wash bhindi by mixing 1 tbs salt in water. Pat dry. This will make the bhujia crispy.

2. Cut bhindis crosswise into small pieces about 2 cm. thick.

3. Heat oil in a wok, put methi and wait for it to turn brown. Then add the bhindi pieces and salt.

4. Stir fry till the bhindi pieces turn golden brown. Remove from heat and serve it with warm paratha or rice.

Aloo bhujia (Potato fry)

Ingredients

Potatoes (medium-sized) – 8
Methi (fenugreek seeds) – ½ tsp
Red chili (dry) small – 1 piece
Turmeric powder – 1 tsp
Oil – 2 tbs
Salt – to taste

Method

1. Wash potatoes, pat dry and cut into small pieces. You can cut them crosswise or lengthwise, make sure that the pieces are uniform in size and thickness.

2. Heat oil in a frying pan, add methi, wait for methi to turn brown then add the red chili piece.

3. When the chili starts to sizzle, add potato pieces with salt and turmeric. Mix well. Turn down heat, cover, but stir intermittently.

4. When potatoes are cooked, remove lid, turn-up the heat and stir till the pieces are uniform in color and slightly crisp.

This bhujia can be served warm with paratha or rice.

Part - 3
Bread, Rice etc.

Litti

Peetha

Pulao

and more ...

Makuni (Sattu Paratha)

Ingredients

Wheat flour – 4 cups
Sattu – 1 cup
Onion (finely chopped) – 2 tbs
Garlic (finely chopped) – 1 tbs
Ginger (finely chopped) –1/2 tbs
Green chili (finely chopped) – 1/4 tbs
Coriander(cilantro leaves chopped) - 1 tbs
Ajwain – 1/4 tsp
Mangrail (kalonji) – 1/4 tsp
Mustard oil or olive oil– 1 tbs
Salt – to taste
Ghee (clarified butter) - 4 tbs.

Method

1. Mix sattu and all other ingredients (except wheat flour), together with two tablespoons water. Knead them for a few minutes so that the flavors assimilate well. Keep this sattu-mixture aside.

2. Make dough of wheat flour. It should be of consistency of bread dough. Cover it with a wet cheese cloth and let sit for about 30 minutes.

3. Divide the dough into 7 equal-sized balls.

4. Roll a ball into a 3-inch diameter circle, put 2 tbs sattu-mixture in the middle and gather all the edges together to make a sattu-filled pouch.

5. Prepare sattu-filled pouches of the remaining dough balls.

6. Carefully, roll each pouch into a round chapati. It will be slightly thick due to the filling.

7. Cook the chapatis on a tava or griddle. You can pan-fry it with a little ghee or cook it as dry chapati (see the note below).

Note: To cook as dry chapati, put a stuffed chapati on the griddle, cook one side then flip it over. Use a paper towel or a cheese cloth to press along the edges while gently rotating the chapati. It will puff up. Make sure that both sides and the edges are cooked thoroughly.

Litti

Ingredients

Wheat flour – 4 cups
Sattu – 2 cups
Onion (finely chopped) – 4 tbs
Garlic (finely chopped) – 4 tbs
Ginger (finely chopped) – 1 tbs
Green chili (finely chopped) – 1 tbs
Coriander(cilantro chopped) – 1 tbs
Ajwain – 1 tsp
Mangrail (kalonji) – 1/2 tsp
Lime juice - 2 tbs
Mustard oil – 1/4 cup or olive oil - 2 tbs
Salt – to taste

Method

1. Keep the wheat flour aside.

2. Mix sattu and all other ingredients together with two tbs water.

3. Knead them for a few minutes so that the flavors assimilate well. Keep this sattu-mixture aside.

4. Make dough of wheat flour. It should be of consistency of bread dough. Cover it with a wet cheese cloth and let sit for about 30 minutes.

5. Divide the dough into 16 equal-sized balls.

6. Press each ball , put 2 tbs sattu-mixture in the middle and gather all the edges together to make a sattu-filled pouch. (See picture on the left.)

7. Roll the pouch by hand evenly into a round ball-like shape.

(Litti contd. from the previous page)

8. Pre-heat oven to 400 F. Arrange the litti balls on a thick cookie sheet and bake for 20 minutes till the color is slightly brown. The litti may develop small cracks as they cook.

Serve warm litti with Aloo chokha and any curried vegetable.

Peetha Chana Dal

Ingredients

Wheat flour – 2 cups
Chana dal (pigeon pea) – 1 cup
Garlic paste – 1 1/2 tbs
Ginger paste – 1 tbs
Green chili (finely chopped) – 1/2 tbs
Coriander (cilantro) chopped – 2 tbs
Turmeric powder – 1 tsp
Cumin seeds – 1/2 tsp
Hing (asafoetida) – 1 pinch
Ghee (clarified butter) – 4 tbs
Salt – to taste

Method

1. Soak chana dal in water for 5-6 hours then rinse it thoroughly and grind it into a thick paste using small amount of water. Mix all the spices and hing into the chana-paste. Keep this mixture aside.

2. Make dough of the wheat flour. Divide it into 8 small balls.

3. Roll a ball into ¼ inch thick chapati. Press in the center. Put 2 tbs chana dal mixture and fold the chapati into half. Press the edges to seal it. This will make one peetha. (See the picture on the opposite page.) Similarly, make pitha of the remaining dough. Brush each peetha will a little ghee.

4. In a steamer, bring water to a boil, arrange the peetha into single layer, cover and cook for 2-3 minutes, uncover and brush with a little ghee, arrange the second layer and repeat the process till all peetha pieces are placed in the steamer.

5. Steam-cook for 20-25 minutes. Insert a knife into a peetha, if the knife comes-out clean the peetha is cooked. Remove from the stove and let it cool. It can be served with coriander chutney.

Variation – Pan-fried Peetha

1. *Cut a cooked peetha into small pieces cross-wise.*

2. *Heat oil in a pan, add rai or mustard seed and curry leaves, let them sizzle. Add the pieces and pan fry them to a golden color.*

These crisp pieces can be served with tomato sauce.

Dal bahri Poori (Chana dal stuffed bread)

Ingredients

Wheat flour – 2 cup
Chana dal – 1 cup
Methi (fenugreek seeds) – 1/2 tsp
Turmeric powder – 1/2 tsp
Chili dry whole – 1 piece
Hing – 1 pinch
Cumin seed – 1tsp
Salt – to taste
Ghee (clarified butter) – 100 ml.
Oil – 1 tbs

Method

1. Soak the dal in water for 6 hours.

2. In the meantime, knead the wheat flour into a dough and set aside.

3. After 6 hours, remove dal from water. Heat oil in a wok, add the hing, fenugreek seeds, and wait for the seeds to turn brown, then add the red chili.

4. Fry for 30 seconds, add the soaked dal and cook till the extra liquid evaporates.

5. In a pressure cooker, add 1/2 cup of water, the dal, turmeric, and salt. Cover and cook for 10 minutes. Let it cool, and then grind the dal into a fine paste.

6. Add cumin seeds to the paste and mix well.

7. Divide the dough of wheat flour into 8 equal parts and make them into small balls. Make a hole in each ball, fill it with the 2 tablespoons dal paste and seal the edges.

Roll the lentil-filled balls into ½ cm thick chapatis. Using a little ghee at a time, pan fry the chapatis to a crisp golden brown color.

It can be served with vegetable curry, raita, and chutney.

Dal pithi (wheat dumplings in cooked lentil)

Ingredients

Masoor dal (red lentil) – 1 cup
Or Moong or Toor/Arhar dal (yellow lentil)

Wheat flour – 1 cup
Cumin seeds – 1/2 tsp
Cumin powder – 1/2 tsp
Turmeric – 1 1/2 tsp
Ginger (finely chopped) – 1 tsp
Garlic (finely chopped) – 1 tbs
Ghee (clarified butter) – 2 tbs
Water – 5 cups
Salt – to taste

Method

1. Rinse the lentil. Cook it in a deep crock-pot with 2 cups water, salt, turmeric, cumin powder and chopped ginger. Keep it aside. (Note: Do not overcook the lentils. It is better if you only half-cook it. When you boil again with the dumplings, the lentils will be cooked thoroughly.)

2. Prepare dough from the wheat flour using water.

3. Make small 1-inch diameter balls from the wheat dough. Roll each dough into 2-inch diameter rounds. Fold each round into the shape of a flower by pinching together the four opposite sides of the edge (shown below), in the middle.

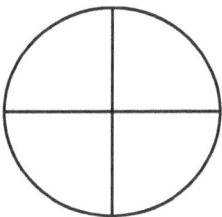

4. The folded dumpling (pithi), will appear like a four-petal flower. See picture on the opposite page. Complete the remaining dumplings and keep them aside.

5. Boil 2 cups water in a saucepan and add it to the cooked lentil and bring the lentil to boil. Add the dumplings, one at a time. Let the dumplings cook, uncovered.

6. If needed, add a cup of boiled water to maintain the consistency of lentil. It will be thick but not watery. The dumplings will firm up when cooked and will not stick together.

7. To season (tadka), heat clarified butter in a deep ladle, add cumin seeds. Wait for it to turn slight brown. Add chopped garlic. Allow garlic to turn brown.

8. Remove ladle from heat and put it into the lentil dumpling pot. Cover the pot . Let the Dal pithi absorb the flavor of tadka.

Serve the seasoned Dal-pithi with any bhujia and a chutney.

Papra (Cheela) Pancake

Ingredients

Besan (Chickpea flour) - 1/2 cup
Rice flour - 1/4 cup
Turmeric powder - 1/2 tsp
Cumin Seed - 1/2 tsp
Ginger paste - 1 tsp
Onion paste - 1 tsp
Carrot grated - 1 tbs
Coriander (cilantro) leaves chopped - 2 tbs
Salt to taste
Oil - 4 tbs

Method

1. Prepare batter by mixing together the chickpea flour and rice flour with enough water.

2. Add the remaining ingredients to the batter along with salt and mix well.

3. Heat 1 teaspoon oil in a heavy-bottom frying pan and add ½ cup batter. Using a spatula, spread the batter in circles to get a shape of pancake. Wait for the top portion to dry (about 1 minute) and flip the pancake over. Cook the other side to nice brown color. You may add a few drops of oil along the edges to make it crispy.

Serve with chutney.

Poori Plain

Ingredients

Wheat flour – 200 grams
Ghee (clarified butter) – 200 ml.
Water – 1 cup

Method

1. Make dough of wheat flour by adding a little water at a time and kneading well.

2. Make small balls of the dough. Roll each of them into ¼ cm thick about 4 inch diameter rounds.

3. Heat ghee in a heavy-bottom pan and deep fry one at a time, to golden brown color.

Kachaouri Savory

Ingredients

Wheat flour – 200 grams
Ajwain – 1/2 tsp
Mangrail (kalonji) – 1/2 tsp
Water – 1 cup
Ghee (clarified) butter – 200 ml.

Method

1. Mix all dry ingredients into wheat flour.

2. Heat 4 tbs ghee and add to the wheat flour, mix well.

3. Using a little water at a time, knead the flour and make a dense dough.

4. Make small balls of the dough. Roll each of them into ¼ cm thick about 3 inch diameter rounds.

5. Heat ghee in a heavy-bottom pan and deep fry one at a time, to golden brown color.

Pulao

Ingredients

Basmati Rice - 1 cup
Black cardamom - 2 pieces
Cloves - 6 pieces
Cinnamon stick - 2 inches long
Javitri (mace) - 4-5 strings
Shyah Jeera (black cumin) - 1 tsp (keep 1/4 tsp aside)
Cumin seeds - 2 tbs
Coriander seeds - 2 tbs
Pepper corn - 1/4 tsp
Tejpatta (bay leaves) - 3 pieces
Green cardamom - 2
Haldi (turmeric) powder - 1/4 tsp
Cashew nuts - 10-12 pieces
Ghee (clarified butter) - 2 tbs
Salt to taste
Water - 4 cups

Method

1. Rinse rice and spread it on a kitchen towel to remove extra water. Leave for 10 minutes.

2. In the meantime, put 4 cups of water in a saucepan, add all whole spices except 1/4 tsp shyah jeera, green cardamom, and bay leaves, and let the water boil till its quantity is reduced to 2 cups. Keep this spice-infused water aside.

3. Heat ghee in a wok. add shyah jeera, green cardamom, and bay leaves, and the rice. Fry till the rice becomes translucent, about 5-6 minutes.

4. Put the fried rice in a deep pot with 2 cups spice-infused water, cashew and salt. Cook till the water is absorbed.

Note: you can cook it in a rice cooker or in a pot or a pressure cooker.

Part - 4
Side dishes

Baingan Chokha

Sattu Chokha

Lauki Raita

and more...

Kachalu (Potatoes with Yogurt)

Ingredients

Potato (boiled, peeled, finely chopped) - 2 cups.
Yogurt plain - 4 cups
Cumin powder (roasted) – 1 tbs
Sugar – ½ tsp
Red chili powder – to taste
Salt – to taste.

Method

1. Whip yogurt so that there are no lumps and it is slightly fluffy.

2. Mix all the spices, salt and potatoes, incorporate properly.

3. If desired, garnish with a few leaves of mint.

Lauki Raita

Ingredients:

Lauki (grated) – 2 cups.
Yogurt plain - 4 cups
Cumin powder (roasted) – 1 ½, tbs
Rai powder (black mustard) – 1 tsp
Sugar – 1 tsp
Red chili powder – to taste
Salt – to taste.

Method

1. Boil grated Lauki in 2 cups of water for 2 minutes till it become soft but not mushy.

2. Squeeze water, and keep the lauki aside.

3. Whip yogurt so that there are no lumps and it is slightly fluffy.

4. Mix all the spices and lauki, incorporate properly.

Aloo Chokha (Mashed potatoes)

Ingredients

Potato – 100 grams
Red chili (dry) -1 piece
Onion (finely chopped) – 2 tbs
Mustard oil – 1 tbs
Salt – to taste

Method

1. Boil, peel and mash the potatoes.

2. Add onion, salt, and oil, mix well.

3. Carefully, roast the chili and crumble it over the potato mixture, mix well.

This mashed potato has a spicy flavor and it serves well with chapati, rice or khitchri.

Sattu Chokha (Spicy)

Ingredients

Sattu – 1/2 cup
Onion (finely chopped) – 1 tbs
Garlic (finely chopped) – 4 cloves
Ginger (finely chopped) – 1 tsp
Green chili (finely chopped) – 1/4 tsp
Coriander(cilantro leaves chopped) - 1 tbs
Ajwain – 1/4 tsp
Mangrail (kalonji) –1/4 tsp
Mustard oil or olive oil – 1 tbs
Lime juice – 1 tbs
Salt – to taste

Method

1. Mix all ingredients together with two tsp water.

2. Knead the mixture for a few minutes so that the flavors assimilate well.

The mixture of this chokha will be crumbly. If it appears to be too dry, more water may be added to get the desired consistency.

Baingan Chokha (Mashed eggplant)

Ingredients

Eggplant – 1 large size (200 grams)
Green chili (finely chopped) -1 tsp
Garlic (minced) – 1 tbs
Coriander (cilantro) leaves – 1 tbs
Mustard oil or Olive oil – 1 tbs
Salt – to taste

Method

1. Make a few slits in the eggplant and broil it in an oven or a grill till the outer skin is evenly charred.

2. Remove the eggplant from heat and let it cool. Peel and remove the charred skin.

3. Mix the pulp of eggplant with the chopped garlic, chili, oil, and salt. Garnish with chopped coriander.

Tamatar Chokha (Mashed Tomatoes)

Ingredients

Tomato – 4 medium-sized
Ginger (finely chopped) -1 tsp
Garlic (finely chopped) – 1 tsp
Coriander (cilantro) leaves chopped – 1 tbs
Mustard oil or Olive oil – 1 tbs
Salt – to taste

Method

1. *Broil or roast the tomatoes till charred. See picture on the opposite page.*

2. *Peel and mash the tomatoes.*

3. *Add all the remaining ingredients, mix well.*

4. *Garnish with green coriander leaves.*

Chana Bajka

Ingredients

Bengal gram (kala chana) soaked – 1 cup
Besan (Gram flour) – 4 tbs
Rice flour – 2 tbs
Onion (finely chopped) – 4 tbs
Garlic paste – 1 1/2 tbs
Green chili (chopped) – 1/2 tsp
Coriander (cilantro leaves) chopped – 2 tbs
Water – 5-6 tbs
Oil – 1/4 cup.
Salt – to taste

Method

1. *Keep ½ cup soaked chana aside.*

2. *Coarsely grind the remaining chana in a blender.*

3. *In a bowl, mix the ½ cup chana with the coarsely ground chana and the remaining ingredients with 2 tbs water.*

4. *Heat oil in a pan and spread the chana mixture into 2-inch round shapes and pan fry on both sides to a golden-brown color.*

Part - 5
Desserts

Laddu

Perakiya

Nariyal Pua

and more...

Pua

Ingredients

Wheat flour – 3/4 cup
Sooji – 1/4 cup
Sugar – 1/2 cup
Cardamom powder – 1/2 tsp
Raisins – 1 tbs
Coconut grated -1 tbs
Fennel seeds – 1/2 tsp
Milk – 1 1/2 cups
Ghee (clarified butter) – 1 1/4 cups

Method

1. *In a large mixing bowl, blend together flour, sugar, sooji, with ½ cup water. The consistency will be of a thick paste. Cover and set it aside for about 4 hours.*

2. *After 4 hours, stir the paste and add the remaining milk to the paste to make a batter. Add all of the remaining spices and mix them well into the batter.*

3. *Heat ghee in a heavy-bottom pan. With a large spoon, drop the prepared batter in the ghee. It will spread like a pancake.*

4. *Keep the heat to medium and fry it to a golden brown color on both sides.*

Sohan Halwa (Sweet Gram Squares)

Ingredients

Chana dal (yellow gram/ pigeon pea) – 300 grams
Khoya (mawa) – 100 grams
Sugar – 150 grams
Ghee (clarified butter) – 100 grams
Cashew nuts (chopped) – 2 tbs
Raisins – 2 tbs
Almonds (chopped) – 2 tbs
Cardamom powder – 1/2 tsp
Milk – 1 cup
Water – 1/2 cup

Method

1. Rinse the dal and soak it in water for 5-6 hours.

2. In a heavy-bottom pot, put the soaked dal with milk and water and cook till the liquids are absorbed and the lentil has softened. (Keep stirring otherwise it will stick to the bottom of the pot and start to burn.)

3. When the cooked dal has cooled down, grind it into a thick paste. You can use a blender.

4. Heat the ghee (clarified butter) in a wok and fry the dal-paste to a golden brown color. When it starts to lump together in a dough-like consistency and appears a little greasy, remove from the wok and set it aside.

5. In the empty wok, make a sugar syrup with ¼ cup water. The syrup will be little sticky, but not too thick.

6. Remove the wok from heat. Add the browned dal-paste, khoya, and cardamom powder into the sugar syrup and mix them well.

7. Bring the wok back to heat, and stir the mixture for another 3-4 minutes till it starts to dry out and leave a little oil along the edges.

8. Remove from heat and spread the mixture on a cookie sheet or tray. Roll it into a uniform 1 inch thick layer, garnish with chopped cashews and almonds.

After the mixture cools, cut it into serving-size square pieces.

Perakiya of khoya (Stuffed Sweet Pastry)

Ingredients

Khoya (mawa) – 100 grams
Maida (all purpose wheat flour)–250 grams
Sugar (powdered) – 50 grams

Raisins – 2 tbs
Almonds (chopped) – 2 tbs
Cardamon powder – ½ tsp

Ghee (clarified butter) – 300 mL.
(Can be substituted with Canola oil or vegetable oil.)

Method

1. Fry the dry khoya in a wok on low heat (no oil is needed.) It will turn crumbly and slight golden. Remove from heat and add the sugar and spices. Keep it aside.

2. Take the maida (flour) and add 8 tbs ghee to it. Mix well so that the maida starts to clump together.

3. Heat 1 cup of water and using about 2 tbs of hot water at a time, make dough of the maida. Divide the dough into 1-inch round balls.

4. Roll a ball into a 4-inch diameter circle. Put 1 tbs of the khoya mixture in the middle of the rolled dough. Apply a little water at the edge of the circle and fold it over (into a half-circle). It will appear crescent-shaped. Seal the edge by pressing it with the pronged-side of a fork. (Or you can pinch and fold forming a twisted pattern along the edges.)

5. Roll the remaining dough-balls, fill, and shape them as above. Keep aside these perakiyas for frying.

6. Heat the remaining ghee in a deep, heavy-bottom wok, keep heat to a medium-low, add two perakiyas at a time and fry them to golden brown color.

Once cooled, the perakiyas can be stored in an air-tight container for 4-5 days or in a refrigerator for up to two weeks.

Gond Laddu

Ingredients

Wheat flour – 250 grams
Sugar (powdered) – 125 grams
Gond (edible char gond) – 50 grams
Khoya (mawa) grated – 150 grams
Cashew (chopped) - 2 tbs
Raisins – 1 Tbs
Walnuts (chopped) – 2 tbs
Almonds (chopped) – 2 tbs
Cardamom powder – 1 tsp
Ghee (clarified butter) – 1 1/4 cups

Method

1. Dry roast the wheat flour in a heavy-bottom wok on low heat. Remove and set it aside.

2. Add 3 tbs of ghee in the empty wok and when it is hot, add the pieces of gond. The pieces will puff-up like a popped corn kernel and become whitish in color. Remove the puffed pieces and grid them into fine powder.

3. In a large bowl, mix the gond powder, sugar, and the remaining ingredients (except the ghee) with the roasted flour. Stir with hand so that the ingredients incorporate well with the wheat flour.

4. Heat the remaining ghee in the wok, take a small batch of the flour-mixture and drizzle a tsp of warm ghee on it. and shape it into a ball.

Make small balls of the remaining mixture using a little ghee at a time. Let is cool then keep in an airtight container.

Narial Pua
(Coconut filled pastry)

Ingredients

Maida (Bleached wheat flower) - 1 cup
Sugar - 1 cup
Coconut (grated) - 1/2 cup
Cardamom powder - 1/4 tsp
Raisins - 1 tsp
Ghee (clarified butter) - 1 1/2 cups
Water - 2 cups

Method

1. To make sugar syrup:
   Add 1 cup water and 1 cup sugar in a heavy-bottom sauce pan and boil it for about 7-8 minutes. Set it aside.

2. To make the filling:
   Mix grated coconut, raisins, and 1/4 cup sugar. Set it aside.

3. To make the pastry dough mix maida with 4 tbs. clarified butter. Make a dough by adding warm water. Knead it well.

4. Divide the dough into 20 pieces. Roll it into 4" diameter rounds. Make 2 separate rounds.

5. Put 1 tsp mixture of the grated coconut filling in the middle of one round and cover it with the other. Press around the edges.

6. Seal the edges by pressing and twisting it so that it makes a pattern. You can also press it with a fork. Make filled pastries of the remaining dough. You will have 10 pastries total.

Heat the remaining ghee in a wok. Keep the heat on medium low and fry the filled pastries in batches.

7. Finishing:
   Dip the fried pastries in the sugar-syrup. Let it cool then serve

Notes

Basic Curry

There are two basic types of curry in Bhojpur style of cooking:

1. Gram Masala Rassa (onion-based curry), and

2. Sarson Rassa (mustard-based curry).

Curried vegetables are usually called 'Tarkari' in traditional language of Bhojpur. A dry vegetable preparation, on the other hand, is called 'Bhujia'. Following are the basic ingredients for the two types of curry.

1. Gram Masala Rassa (onion-based curry)

Onion paste, garlic paste, ginger paste, corinader powder, cumin powder, turmeric powder, and chili powder. Oil is seasoned with cumin seed then the onion, garlic and ginger paste are fried before adding the dry spices. Once the spices are fried to a golden-brown color, vegetable and water are added and cooked to get the desired consistency.

2. Sarson Rassa (mustard-based curry)

Ginger paste, garlic paste, coriander powder, turmeric powder, mustard powder, and chili powder. Oil is seasoned with fenugreek seeds (Methi), and chopped tomatoes are added along with water to prepare the gravy. Dry mango powder (Amchoor) is added at the end.

Notes

Notes

www.ingramcontent.com/pod-product-compliance
Lightning Source LLC
Chambersburg PA
CBHW050815090426
42736CB00021B/3459